THE GATES OF SHALMANESER

OXFORD
PLATES AND LETTERPRESS
PRINTED AT THE UNIVERSITY PRESS
BY HORACE HART M.A.

BRONZE RELIEFS

FROM

THE GATES OF SHALMANESER

KING OF ASSYRIA B.C. 860-825

EDITED BY

L. W. KING, M.A., LITT.D.

ASSISTANT KEEPER OF EGYPTIAN AND ASSYRIAN ANTIQUITIES

WITH EIGHTY PLATES

LONDON
PRINTED BY ORDER OF THE TRUSTEES
SOLD AT THE BRITISH MUSEUM, AND BY
LONGMANS & CO., 39 PATERNOSTER ROW; BERNARD QUARITCH, 11 GRAFTON STREET,
NEW BOND STREET, W.; ASHER & CO., 10 BEDFORD STREET, COVENT GARDEN;
AND HUMPHREY MILFORD, OXFORD UNIVERSITY PRESS, AMEN CORNER, E.C.
1915

CENTRAL LIBRARY
THE BRITISH MUSEUM
WITHDRAWN

PREFACE

THE present volume contains a complete reproduction in collotype of the hammered and engraved bronze bands which ornamented a pair of wooden gates set up at the entrance to a palace of Shalmaneser, King of Assyria B.C. 860–825. In it are also included reproductions of two bronze bands from a smaller pair of gates, which we now know were made by Ashur-naṣir-pal, from whom Shalmaneser inherited the palace. The scenes upon these larger gates illustrate the principal incidents of a series of campaigns which were conducted by Shalmaneser during the first thirteen years of his reign, and the scenes upon the bands from the smaller gates are also of a military character.

In the year 1876 the natives of the district of Nimrûd (the Calah of Genesis x. 11) discovered these bands, and some fragments of them were dispatched to London and Paris for examination by experts and sale. In the following year the Trustees of the British Museum sent the late Mr. Hormuzd Rassam to Môṣul to continue their excavations at Kuyûnjik. Whilst there he acquired for the Trustees the bronze reliefs published herein, as well as a stone altar, and a stone coffer containing two inscribed stone tablets of Ashur-naṣir-pal. These tablets commemorated the building of the city of Imgur-Bêl, and the founding of the Temple of Makhir within it. Therefore it was believed that the bronze gates came from the doorway of that temple. All these objects, according to the native stories, were found in the mound near the village of Tell Balâwât, which is situated on the east or left bank of the Tigris, from 15 to 20 miles south-east of Môṣul. When I was in Assyria in 1888 I endeavoured to acquire any further fragments which might possibly be in the hands of natives, but it was not until I was in Mesopotamia on my third Mission in 1890–1 that I was able to visit Balâwât. Having examined the mound I found it impossible to believe that this insignificant site could have contained an Assyrian temple. In 1901

Mr. L. W. King was sent to Assyria to examine Assyrian sites, including Balâwât, with a view to further excavations, and in his official report he expressed a similar opinion arrived at independently. Meanwhile the Bronze Gates have become commonly known as the 'Gates of Balâwât'.

Matters stood thus until the present publication was undertaken, when it became necessary to examine the inscriptions systematically. In the course of this work Mr. King obtained evidence which showed that the smaller gates at all events, stood in a palace of Ashur-naṣir-pal. This fact finally disproves the statements of the natives about their place of origin, for it is quite impossible that Tell Balâwât contained an Assyrian Palace as well as a temple. Therefore we must conclude that the site of Imgur-Bêl is still problematical, and that the place where the bronze reliefs published herein were found has not yet been ascertained.

The importance of the Bronze Gates of Shalmaneser for the study of ancient art cannot be overestimated, and it was necessary that accurate reproductions of them should be available for students. The green-tinted photographs published under the title 'The Bronze Ornaments from the Palace Gates of Balawat', London 1880–1902, were made from plaster casts much restored, and a great deal of the sharpness of outline of the original disappeared in the moulding. The reproductions in the present volume have been photographed direct from the metal, and though the scale has, necessarily, been reduced a little less than one-half, the smallest detail of costume, &c. is now apparent.

Full descriptions of the bronze reliefs are given in the Introduction, and short labels have been printed on the Plates to facilitate their use. A complete translation of the cuneiform text, engraved on the bronze sheathing which protected the edges of the gates of Shalmaneser, has also been given. All these are the work of Mr. L. W. King, M.A., Litt.D., Assistant Keeper in the Department.

E. A. WALLIS BUDGE.

Department of Egyptian and Assyrian
Antiquities, British Museum,
January 21, 1915.

CONTENTS

INTRODUCTION

THE thirteen bronze Bands, which are reproduced on Plates I–LXXVII, formed part of the decoration of a massive pair of gates from an entrance to a palace of Shalmaneser III, and they represent the finest example of work in *bronze repoussé* which has survived from so early a period. They are said to have been found by an Arab, while engaged in digging a grave in the mound near Balâwât,[1] a village about fifteen miles south-east of Môṣul and some nine miles north-east of Nimrûd. A fragment of the engraved bronze was sent to this country, and, after his return to Môṣul in 1877, the late Mr. Hormuzd Rassam recovered the greater part of the bands, as well as portions of the other bronze fittings of the gates, for the British Museum. Ten small fragments, including a part of the inscription, were sent by a dealer in Môṣul to Monsieur Gustave Schlumberger of Paris, who purchased them;[2] one of these belongs to the missing portion of Band VIII (see Pl. XLIII). Twenty other small fragments, which have since been joined up to form seven separate pieces, were acquired in Paris for the Louis de Clercq Collection, and have now passed into the possession of M. le Comte Louis de Boisgelin;[3] one of these also restores a further portion of Band VIII. And there are two separate fragments in the Museum at Constantinople.[4] But all these are comparatively small fragments, and, with the exception of those from Band VIII (see above), are apparently from

[1] Cf. Rassam, *Trans. Soc. Bibl. Arch.*, vol. vii (1882), p. 45; but see below, p. 11.

[2] See Lenormant, *Gazette Archéologique*, vol. iv (1878), Pl. 22–4, for seven of the reliefs, reproduced half-scale, and the inscription-fragment, of which the latter is republished in *Collection de Clercq*, vol. ii, Pl. 28 (*bis*), No. 1; and Unger, *Zum Bronzetor von Balawat*, p. 8 f., Pl. II, for the two remaining relief-fragments of this group.

[3] See *Collection de Clercq*, vol. ii, Pl. 29–33, Nos. 6–25, reproduced actual size; four small fragments of the inscription are given on Pl. 28 (*bis*), Nos. 2–5.

[4] Cf. Unger, *op. cit.*, p. 9, Pl. II. Three small fragments appear also to have remained in Mr. Rassam's possession.

three Bands only. The British Museum, on the other hand, possesses thirteen nearly complete bands, and other bronze fittings, as well as parts of the bronze coverings of a pair of smaller gates, of which specimens are given as an Appendix on Plates LXXVIII–LXXX. These smaller gates have hitherto been ascribed to Shalmaneser, but it is now certain that they were set up in the palace by Shalmaneser's father, Ashur-naṣir-pal (B.C. 885–860).[1] From a study of them in comparison with the larger gates it will be seen that the Assyrian metal-workers made a considerable advance in technical skill and composition during the interval. A series of photographs of the bands from the larger gates was published by the Society of Biblical Archaeology from a partly restored plaster cast;[2] the collotype plates of both sets of gates in the present volume have been taken direct from the bronze itself.

Each door of the larger pair of gates measured about 6 ft. in width and over 20 ft. in height. They were made of wood, probably cedar, and the flat portion of each was fixed to a massive post or cylindrical shaft, 18 in. in diameter, the lower end of which projected below the bottom of the door and was shod by a heavy bronze pivot working in a stone socket. The posts or shafts were surmounted by great caps and knobs of hollow bronze, and they moved within bronze collars which were fixed into the sides of the doorway near the top. Across the flat portion of each door and around the attached shaft the bronze bands were nailed, separated from each other by blank spaces showing the wood of the door. The metal of which the bands are made is only about $\frac{1}{16}$ in. in thickness and was obviously intended for decoration, not to strengthen the gates against attack. But the end of each band, at the centre of the doorway, was covered by a sheathing of thicker bronze, which bound the edge of each door from top to bottom. Upon each of these bronze edgings the Gate-Inscription[3] was engraved in duplicate.

If we may accept the tradition that the two pairs of gates were found

[1] See below, p. 15 f.

[2] *The Bronze Ornaments of the Palace Gates of Balawat*; Introductions by Samuel Birch and Walter de Grey Birch; descriptions, &c., by T. G. Pinches (1880–1902). A later study of the gates has been published by Billerbeck and Delitzsch, *Die Palasttore Salmanassars II aus Balawat*, in the *Beiträge zur Assyriologie*, Bd. VI, Heft 1 (1908), and has been supplemented by Unger, *Zum Bronzetor von Balawat* (1912).

[3] See below, p. 17 ff.

together, their difference in size may perhaps be explained by the fact that they closed the outer and the inner opening of a double gateway, such as has been found in the Anu and Adad Temple at Ashur.[1] In that case the palace in which they were set up had been inherited by Shalmaneser from his father, who had decorated the inner doors with bands of bronze reliefs, leaving his son to complete the decoration of the pair which closed the outer entrance. The fact that we may now identify the building in which they were set up as a royal palace[2] adds to the difficulty of accepting the original story of their discovery, which has been felt by all who have visited Balâwât. That so insignificant a mound should have covered the temple of Makhir and the city of Imgur-Bêl was hardly credible; that it should also have contained a royal palace reduces the story to an absurdity. We may conclude that the native finders of the gates took good care to conceal the actual site of their discovery.[3] The scenes upon the larger doors are devoted entirely to Shalmaneser's military expeditions, while hunting-scenes are included on Ashur-naṣir-pal's smaller pair of doors.

Each bronze band from the larger gates measures some 8 ft. in length and about 11 in. in height. On each the engraved scenes are arranged in two registers between plain bands, edged by line-borders and ornamented with rosettes. The beaded circle of each rosette is stamped in the bronze around each nail-hole, the heads of the nails, used for fastening the bronze to the woodwork, forming the centres of the rosettes. The process by which the reliefs were produced seems to have been the following. The design was first engraved in outline on the bronze, which was then bedded face downwards in bitumen. In consequence of the thinness of the metal the engraved outline would show through, so that it would have been a comparatively simple task for the engraver to mould the figures by hammering out the bronze as it lay on its yielding bed. There was probably little, if any, touching up with a graver after the figures had been rendered in relief. That this was the process is clear from the fact that occasionally details are left

[1] Cf. Andrae, *Der Anu-Adad-Tempel in Assur* (1909), p. 48 ff. [2] See below, p. 15.

[3] Indeed, the gates need not have been found with Ashur-naṣir-pal's coffer and tablet (cf. Budge and King, *Annals*, p. 167 f., n. 2); they may have been found at Nimrûd and afterwards buried by their discoverers in the neighbouring mound of Balâwât. The *provenance* of the stone coffer and tablet remains even more uncertain.

engraved only and have not been hammered into relief. The flat appearance of the scenes after engraving and before the process of hammering may be seen from two figures on Plate XXI. On the other hand, the inscriptions in the field of the registers were evidently added after the plates had been fastened to the doors. For the surface of the bronze has here been left indented, which would not have been the case had they been engraved at the same time as the figures.

The bands may be recognized as having belonged to the right-hand or left-hand door, by the position of the circular portions which enclosed the shafts or posts. Of the thirteen bands in the British Museum, seven (Bands I–IV, VIII, XI, and XIII) belonged to the right-hand door; and six (Bands V–VII, IX, X, and XII) belonged to that on the left. Of the remaining three bands,[1] ends of which have been recovered, one is from the right-hand and two from the left-hand door. Thus each door must have carried at least eight bands. The thirteen bands in the British Museum are here published in the chronological order of the scenes engraved upon them. The following table gives the subject of each band, the date of the expedition represented, and the texts [2] relating to it:

Band.	*Date of Expedition.*	*Region.*	*Principal places.*	*Texts.*
I.	860 B. C.	Armenia.	Lake Van; Sugunia.	Mon., Obv., ll. 23–7.
II.	860 ,,	Armenia.	Cities of Urartu.	Mon., Obv., l. 25.
III.	859 ,,	Phoenicia.	Tyre, Sidon; Khazazu.	Gate Inscr., II. ll. 3–5; Mon., Rev., ll. 5–7, 10–12; and cf. Bl. Ob., ll. 26–31.
IV.	858 ,,	Northern Syria.	Dabigu.	Mon., Rev., ll. 13–18; Bl. Ob., ll. 32–5.
V.	858 ,,	Northern Syria.	Unḳu.	Mon., Rev., ll. 21–4, and possibly ll. 24–7.

[1] See above, p. 9 f.

[2] For a translation of the Gate-Inscription, see below, pp. 17 ff.; and for the text, see Pinches in *Gates of Balawat*, Appendix, pp. 1 ff., and cf. Delitzsch, *Beiträge z. Assyr.*, VI, i, pp. 133 ff. and Unger, *Zum Bronzetor von Balawat*, pp. 16 ff.; for the Monolith-Inscription, see Rawlinson, *Cun. Inscr. West. Asia*, vol. III, pl. 7 f.; for the Black Obelisk, see Abel and Winckler, *Keilschrifttexte*, pp. 7 ff.; and for the Bull-Inscription, see Layard, *Cuneiform Inscriptions*, pl. 12–16, 46 f., and Delitzsch, *op. cit.*, pp. 144 ff.

Band.	*Date of Expedition.*	*Region.*	*Principal places.*	*Texts.*
VI.	858 B. C.	Northern Syria.	Carchemish.	Mon., Rev., ll. 18–20, 27–9.
VII.	857 „	Armenia.	Urartu ; Gilzani.	Gate Inscr., II, l. 5—III, l. 3; Mon., Rev., ll. 47–54, 60–2; Bl. Ob., ll. 42–4; Bull Inscr., ll. 55–60.
VIII.	855 „	North-East Mesopotamia.	Shubru.	Bl. Ob., ll. 52–4; Bull Inscr., ll. 66–7.
IX.	854 „	Syria (Hamath).	Pargâ, Adâ ; Ḳarḳar.	Mon., Rev., ll. 87–101; Bl. Ob., ll. 57–66; Bull Inscr., ll. 71–4.
X.	853 „	Source of Tigris.	Kulisi.	Bl. Ob., ll. 67–72; Bull Inscr., ll. 75–7.
XI.	851 „	South Babylonia.	Bit-Dakuri.	Gate Inscr., IV, l. 1–VI, l. 8; Bl. Ob., ll. 83–4; Bull Inscr., ll. 82–4.
XII.	850 „	Northern Syria.	Arnê.	Bl. Ob., ll. 85–6; Bull Inscr., ll. 84–7, and, possibly, ll. 90 f., 94 f.
XIII.	849 „	Syria (Hamath).	Ashtamaku.	Bl. Ob., ll. 87–8; Bull Inscr., ll. 91–2.

The subject of each Band can be identified with certainty by means of the short inscriptions engraved in the field above the figures. In the 'Description of Plates'[1] those relating to each Band are grouped together and the description is arranged under the three headings: (1) Texts, (2) Upper Register, and (3) Lower Register. Under the first of these headings the short labels engraved in the field of both registers are translated, and the information on the campaign, which is furnished by our texts, is summarized or quoted. Under the other two headings short descriptions are given of the scenes in the two registers. Most of the details explain themselves, and the descriptions are confined in the main to identifying the separate sections with the records. The few conventions employed are readily recognizable, such as the representation of mountains, or rocky country, by means of superimposed lozenges. It may further be noted that the king may always be identified by his peaked conical head-dress, the mark of royalty; and that foreign prisoners or deputations, when introduced into

[1] See below, p. 21 ff.

the royal presence, are invariably preceded by an Assyrian officer, who raises one hand and points to them, thus separating them from the Assyrian Court officials at the head of each procession.

One of the most interesting features of the engraving consists in the attempt at portraying different ethnic types and national costumes among the captives and tributary peoples represented on the monument. These may be classified into three main groups, the Western, the Northern, and the Southern, according to their geographical distribution. Under the first and largest of the groups, the Western, may be mentioned the Phoenicians of Tyre and Sidon on Band III (Upper Register); the Syrian Hittites of Carchemish on Band VI; the Hamathites on Bands IX and XIII; and other mixed tribes of Northern Syria, in which Aramean, Hittite, and Phoenician strains were blended in varying degrees, such as the Patinians of Khazazu on Band III (Lower Register), the Unḳians on Band V (Lower Register), and the subjects of Akhuni of the Adini-tribe on Band IV. The Gusians of Arnê and other cities on Band XII had been long settled in the West, but they may have presented closer affinities to the Urartian, or Northern, groups of peoples. This second group includes the Urartians themselves, inhabitants of the Armenian highlands, who are portrayed on Bands I, II, and VII (Upper Register); the Gilzanians, who occupied the western shore of Lake Urmiah, on Band VII (Lower Register); the Shubrians, to the south and south-west of Diarbekr, on Band VIII; and probably the inhabitants of Kulisi, in the neighbourhood of the 'Source of the Tigris' to the east of that city, on Band X. The third, or Southern, group comprises one race only, the Chaldeans of Bît-Dakuri, who are depicted on Band XI.

The engraving of the bands from the larger gates has not been carried out by a single hand. To the principal engraver may be assigned Bands I–III, V–VII, and IX–XI. Any one who will examine the style and workmanship of these nine bands will at once recognize that Bands IV, VIII, XII, and XIII are not his work. Of these, by far the least skilful is Band VIII, with its awkward figures, its tumble-down cities, and its perfunctory lozenge-work. In the size and treatment of its figures Band IV resembles Band VIII, but the work is far more skilfully carried out; and its engraver, when not reproducing a conventionalized type, shows keen observation and some originality. Notice, for example, the attitude of the saddle-mule on Plate XXIII, or the attempted perspective on Plate XX with its representation of figures surrounding the king upon a low hill or mound. Bands XII and XIII may be classified together as presenting a certain general resemblance, but, of the two, Band XIII is by far the more advanced in treatment. From the technical standpoint it is perhaps the most interesting band in the whole series. The realistic treatment of figures in violent motion is remarkable in the chariot pursuit on Plate LXXII, as in the charge of the royal chariot on Plate LXXIV. Moreover, the manner in which chariots and figures are superimposed marks a great advance in composition upon the comparative isolation of figures in other bands.

The inclusion of such apparently careless work as that on Band VIII is easily explicable. This and the other less finished bands were evidently fixed across the upper part of the doors, from ten to fourteen feet above eye-level, and any elaborate finish to the workmanship would have been wasted labour. That this explanation is the true one is proved by another characteristic of the less finished bands, which has hitherto been left unexplained,—the disproportionate height of the figures on those bands. So far from being due to carelessness or want of skill, the great height of these figures was most carefully designed, so that, when seen from below, they should range with the figures in the lower bands and appear to the spectator on the ground-level as of normal proportions.[1]

On Plates LXXVIII–LXXX two Bands from the smaller Gates of Ashur-naṣir-pal are published as an Appendix. A complete publication of this monument will only be possible after all the bands have been carefully cleaned and the fragments re-examined. The two bands here selected are the only ones on which the designs may be made out, as the result of the cleaning they underwent at the time of their discovery. That the gate which they adorned stood in the entrance of a palace of Ashur-naṣir-pal is certain from the first inscription on Band I, which begins, like so many of

[1] It is clear that the bands were not arranged upon the gates in chronological order. As they were designed for decorative effect, it is obvious that their arrangement would have been determined by the character of the reliefs upon them, with little, if any, reference to the relative order of the campaigns.

Ashur-naṣir-pal's texts, with the words 'Palace of Ashur-naṣir-pal', followed by the royal genealogy. The subjects on the bands selected both relate to conquests of Ashur-naṣir-pal, but other bands are engraved with striking episodes from royal lion-hunts. Like the scenes themselves, the inscriptions on most of them will be decipherable when further cleaning has been attempted.

Each door of this smaller pair of gates measured about 3 ft. 4½ in. in width, the flat portion of the door measuring about 2 ft. 4 in., while the cylindrical shaft to which it was attached measured just over a foot in diameter. The bands are from 6½ in. to 7 in. in height, and each contains a single register between plain bands, edged with line-borders and rosettes, as in the larger gates of Shalmaneser. At the top and bottom of each register additional borders are introduced, decorated with a palmette above each nail-head. Of these additional borders the lower one furnishes the ground level for the composition, but the upper one is cut into occasionally by projecting spears, towers, &c. The thickness of the bronze employed for the bands varies, and the technique and composition are not so advanced as on Shalmaneser's gates. It may be added that the figures are on a larger scale than those in Shalmaneser's double registers.

THE GATE-INSCRIPTION OF SHALMANESER

Col. I, (1) Shalmaneser, the great King, the mighty King, King of the world, King of [Assyria, the son of Ashur-naṣir-pal, King of the world, King of Assyria, the son of Tukulti-Ninib, King of the world, King of] Assyria, the strong hero, who in the four quarters of the world (2) gives no pardon, who conquers rebellion [. . . . .] to whose hand all the quarters of the world are entrusted, who crushes (3) those who submit not to Ashur, the mighty flood [. . . . .], in whose hands [Ashur] has set the ends of the lands, King of the quarters of the world, (4) (who is covered with) splendour, who fears not opposition [. . . . ., under the yoke of] whose dominion mighty ruthless kings (5) as far as the setting of the sun have humbled themselves [. . . . .], Shalmaneser, the true shepherd, the priest of Ashur, (6) the powerful. At that time when Ashur, the great lord, [my lord, ... had uttered my name for rule] over the peoples, and had crowned me with the exalted crown of dominion,

Col. II, (1) and the weapon, the sceptre, and the mace for all peoples had entrusted to my hand, and I was proceeding with the help of Ashur, the great lord, my lord, and of the god that loves my priesthood, and when all the lands and the wooded mountains to their whole extent (2) he had placed within my grasp: I, Shalmaneser, the mighty King, the Sun of all peop[les . . . . .], who has conquered from the Sea of the land of Nairi[1] and the Sea of the land of Zamûa,[2] which is over against it (?), and the Great Sea of Amurrû,[3] overwhelmed the land of Khatti in its whole extent, (so that it became) like a mound left by the deluge. (3) Forty-four thousand, four hundred strong warriors I carried away from their lands, and as inhabitants of my own land I coun[ted them . . . . .]. My lordly splendour I poured out over the land of Khatti. In my passage to the sea I fashioned

[1] *I. e.*, Lake Van. [2] *I. e.*, Lake Urmiah. [3] *I. e.*, the Mediterranean.

a great image of my lordliness, and I set it up beside the image of Ankhirbe. (4) The cities beside my path I destroyed, I ravaged, I burned with fire [. . . . .] I marched to the Great Sea; I washed my weapons in the Great Sea, I offered sacrifices to my gods. The tribute of all the kings (5) of the sea-coast I received. I fashioned a great image of my lordliness, and the heroic deeds which I had done by the sea I inscribed thereon, and I set it up beside the sea. (6) From the land of Enzi to the land of Daiâni, from Daiâni t[o (the land of Tumme, from Tumme to) Arṣashkun I conquered. Arṣashkun, the royal city of Ara]me, the Urartian, I captured, I destroyed, I ravaged, I burned with fire. While I tarried in the city of Arṣashkun, Aramu, the Urartian, put his trust in the multitude of his forces,

Col. III, (1) and he summoned all his troops together. To wage war and battle he advanced against me. I defeated him, I smote his soldiers, three thousand of his fighting-men I laid low with the sword. With the blood of his warriors (2) I filled the broad plain. His battle-equipment, his royal treasure, his chargers I took from him. To save his life he climbed a steep mountain. The broad land of Ḳutê I laid waste like the Plague-god. From the city of Arṣashkun to the land of Gilzâni, (3) from Gilzâni to the land of Khubushkia like Adad, the inundator, I roared over them; the terror of my rule I brought upon the land of Urarṭu. Akhuni, the son of Adini, who from the time of the kings, my fathers, (4) had established dominion and power, at the beginning of my reign I shut up in his city; I ravaged his crops, I hewed down his plantations. To save his life he crossed the Euphrates; Shîtamrat, a mountain peak which hung like a cloud from heaven, (5) he made his stronghold. In the second year I went down after him, I stormed the peak of the mountain. My warriors swooped upon them like the bird-god Zû. Seventeen thousand, five hundred of his troops I carried off; Akhuni with his troops, his gods, his chariots, (6) and his horses I took into my possession; I brought them to my city of Ashur; with the [peoples][1] of my land I counted them.

Col. IV, (1) In the eponymy of Shamash-bêl-uṣur, in the time of Marduk-shum-iddina, King of Kardaniash,[2] Marduk-bêl-usâte, his brother,

[1] It is probable that *nišê* should here be read for *bîtâti*. [2] *I. e.*, Babylonia.

revolted against him. They divided the land into two camps. Marduk-shum-iddina sent (2) his messenger to Shalmaneser that he should help him. Shalmaneser, the strong, the terrible, whose help is Ninib, took the road; to march to Akkad he gave the command. To the city of Zaban I drew nigh;[1] sacrifices before Adad, my lord, (3) I offered. I departed from Zaban, and to the city of Mê-turnat I drew nigh. The city I stormed, I captured; I slew its inhabitants, I carried off its spoil. From Mê-turnat I departed, and to the city of Gannanate (4) I drew nigh. Marduk-bêl-usâte, the usurping king, who had no knowledge of the way he should go, to wage war and battle came out against me. I defeated him, I slew his people, I shut him up in his city. His crops (5) I carried off; I hewed down his plantations; I dammed up his canal. On a second expedition, in the eponymy of Bêl-bunâia, on the 20th of Nisan, I departed from Nineveh; I crossed the Upper (6) and the Lower Zab, I drew nigh to Lakhiri. The city I stormed, I captured; I slew its inhabitants, I carried off its spoil. From Lakhiri

Col. V, (1) I departed, and to the city of Gannanate I drew nigh. Marduk-bêl-usâte came forth like a fox from a hole. To the mountain of Iasubi he set his face; the city of Arman (2) he took as his stronghold. Gannanate I captured; I slew its inhabitants, I carried off its spoil. I went up into the mountains after him; I shut him into the city of Arman. I stormed the city, I captured it; its inhabitants (3) I slew, I carried off its spoil. Marduk-bêl-usâte I laid low with the sword, and of the rebels, who were with him, I left not one remaining. After Marduk-shum-iddina had conquered his enemies and Shalmaneser, (4) the mighty King, had seen the fulfilment of his desires, he reverenced the word of the great lord Marduk. Shalmaneser, King of Assyria, gave the word to march to Babylon. He arrived at Cuthah, the city of the hero of the gods, (5) the exalted Nergal; in the door of the temple he humbly prostrated himself and he presented his victim for sacrifice; he gave rich gifts. He entered Babylon, the meeting-place of heaven and earth, the seat of life. (6) He went up to Esagila, the palace of the gods, the dwelling of the King of All.

[1] Abrupt changes from the third to the first person are not uncommon in Assyrian royal inscriptions.

In the presence of Bêl and Bêlit he appeared cast down with fear (?), as he directed [his] steps. His exalted sacrifice, his pure offering, in Esagila

Col. VI, (1) he set in abundance. The temples of Esagila and of Babylon he caused to receive his pure offering. He took the road to (2) Borsippa, the city of the hero of the gods, the exalted son (?), the mighty; he entered Ezida, [the house of des]tinies (?), the house of his sure decision. He humbled himself, and in the presence of Nabû and Nanâ, (3) the gods, his lords, he reverently directed his steps. Mighty oxen, fat sheep he presented in abundance. The temples of Borsippa and Ezida in like manner (4) he caused to receive libations. For the inhabitants of Babylon and Borsippa, the servants under the protection of the great gods, he made a feast and he gave them bread and wine, he clothed them in brightly coloured garments, and with rich gifts (5) he presented them. After the great gods had looked with joy upon Shalmaneser, the mighty King, the King of Assyria, had . . . . . his countenance, had received the . . . . . of his heart and . . . . ., and had heard his prayers, I departed from Babylon and to the land of Chaldea (6) I went down. To Baḳâni, the fortress of Adini, the son of Dakuri, I drew nigh. The city I stormed, I captured, many of its inhabitants I slew; their heavy spoil, their oxen and their sheep I carried off; the city I destroyed, I ravaged, I burned with fire. From Baḳâni I departed, I crossed the Euphrates with him, I drew nigh to Enzudi, (7) the royal city of Adini. As for Adini, the son of Dakuri, fear before the splendour of the great lord Marduk overwhelmed him, and his [tribute (?), ...], silver, gold, bronze, lead, iron, [. . . . . and iv]ory I received from him. While I tarried near (?) the sea, I received the tribute of Iakini, King of the Sea-land, (8) and of Mushallim-Marduk, son of Ukani, silver, gold, lead, bronze, ... and elephants' hide.

DESCRIPTION OF PLATES

PLATES I–VI.

BAND I. CAMPAIGN IN ARMENIA, 860 B.C.

Texts: The inscription in the field of the upper register (Pl. I f.) reads: 'I set up an image on the shore of the Sea of Nairi;[1] I made offerings to my gods.' That on the field of the lower register (Pl. II f.) reads: 'I captured Suguni[a], the city of Arame of Urartu.' These two events, the dedication of the royal image near Lake Van and the capture of Sugunia, were the most striking episodes in Shalmaneser's Armenian campaign of 860 B.C. The Monolith-Inscription, Obv., ll. 23–27, gives the following record of them; in it the capture of Sugunia precedes the dedication of the rock-image, which commemorated the successful completion of the campaign: 'From Khubushkia I departed, and to Sugunia, the stronghold of Arame, I drew nigh. The city I stormed, I captured; their numerous inhabitants I slew; its spoil I carried off. A pile of heads over against his city I heaped up. Fourteen cities, which were round about it, I burned with fire. From Sugunia I departed and I marched to the Sea of Nairi. I washed my weapons in the sea; I made sacrifices to my gods. At that time I made an image in my own likeness; the glory of the lord Ashur, the prince my lord, and the might of my power I wrote thereon. Beside the sea I set it up.'

Upper Register: *Dedication of Shalmaneser's image on the shore of Lake Van.* The king's image (Pl. I) was carved in the living rock, a fact the engraver has indicated by placing it upon four rows of lozenges, intended conventionally to represent mountains. A soldier, standing on a rock near the image, is throwing the legs of an ox, dismembered as a sacrificial victim, into the lake, where they are being seized by the divine monsters of the deep; another soldier drags the ox's head towards the water. Before the image are two royal standards, a table for offerings, a tall incense-burner and a water-pot. The king, wearing the conical head-dress with the small peak, the mark of royalty, is pouring out a libation. He is accompanied by priests and musicians; the former carry offerings heaped on a dish and wine in rhytons ending in animals' heads. The bulls and rams, which are being driven forward by a priest and a soldier (Pl. II), are victims for the sacrifice. This half of the scene is closed by the royal chariot, in which the king had arrived at the place

[1] *I. e.*, Lake Van.

in the hills above the lake, where his image had been sculptured. The right half of the register (Pl. III–VI) represents the escort of chariots, cavalry, and infantry, which accompanied the king across the hills. In one division of the fortified camp (Pl. VI) is the royal pavilion; in the other bread is being prepared and baked.

Lower Register: *The storming and capture of Sugunia.* The city of Sugunia (Pl. III) is being attacked from both sides. The soldiers engaged in storming the walls are clad in mail, as are the shield-bearers who protect the ranks of archers from the arrows of the garrison. Behind the archers are chariots held in reserve (Pl. I f.) and a circular fortified camp. In the right half of the register (Pl. III–VI) prisoners from the captured town are being led before a high Assyrian officer. They consist of boys, youths, and warriors, and, with the exception of the boys, all are yoked and bound. The status of the warriors is shown by the close-fitting crested helmets, which they are represented as still wearing.

PLATES VII–XII.

BAND II. CAMPAIGN IN ARMENIA, 860 B.C.

Texts: That this band, like that which precedes it, refers to the Armenian campaign of 860 B.C. is certain from the inscription in the field of the upper register (Pl. VII f.) which reads: 'Smiting of [. . . . .] of the land of Urartu.' It may be taken to illustrate the burning of the fourteen cities, which were round about Sugunia (cf. Monolith-Inscription, Obv., l. 25, translated above, p. 21).

Upper Register: *The sack and burning of an Urartian city.* The city (Pl. VIII) is seen with flames rising above its massive walls and towers. It stands in a position of natural strength among the mountains, and in the plain below Assyrian soldiers are hewing down its date-plantations. An outlying village, or fortress (Pl. VII f.), has been captured and some of its defenders impaled on the walls; the heads of others are nailed to the towers. A massive corn-jar, part of the spoil from the city, is being removed on a four-wheeled truck (Pl. VII). In Plates IX–XI Assyrians in chariots, under Shalmaneser's leadership, and others on foot are slaughtering Urartians with bow and sword, while in Plate XI f. fresh Urartian troops are seen advancing into battle from the mountains.

Lower Register: *The storming and capture of an Urartian city.* The city (Pl. IX) is very similar to that in the upper register (Pl. VIII). Half of it is represented as still holding out against a storming party; the flames which rise from the other half are an indication of its fate after capture. On Plates VII–IX are the successive lines of the Assyrian investment, while on Plate VII Urartian warriors are being shot down by Assyrian cavalry. With the yoked prisoners and their captors on Plates X–XII, cp. Band I (Pl. IV f., lower register).

PLATES XIII–XVIII.

BAND III. CAMPAIGN IN PHOENICIA, 859 B.C.

Texts: The inscription in the field of the upper register (Pl. XIII f.) reads: 'The tribute of the ships of the men of Tyre and Sidon I received.' That in the field of the lower register (Pl. XVI) reads: 'The smiting of the city of Khazazu.' The Great Inscription on the gates, Col. II, ll. 3–5, refers to this campaign, recording that Shalmaneser received 'the tribute of the kings of the sea-coast', and that he made sacrifices on the coast and set up an image of himself beside the sea.[1] This account may be supplemented from the Monolith-Inscription; Rev., ll. 5–7 read: 'To the great cities of the Patinians I [drew nigh . . . . .]. The upper [cities] of the land of Amurrû and of the Western Sea, I overwhelmed like mounds in the track of a storm. The tribute of the kings of the sea-coast I received. On the coast of the broad sea I marched righteously and in triumph.' Three lines lower down Shalmaneser records his departure from the Mediterranean coast, and he refers to Khazazu among the next group of cities he sacked, ll. 10–12 reading: 'From the sea I [went down . . . . .]. The cities of Taiâ, Khazazu, Nulia, and Butâmu of the Patinians I captured. Two thousand, eight hundred of [their] fighting-men I slew; fourteen thousand, six hundred I carried away as prisoners.'

Upper Register: *The tribute of Tyre and Sidon.* On the left of Plate XIII is the fortified city of Tyre, on its rocky island off the Syrian coast. Tribute is being carried across to the mainland in boats, which, as they near the shore, are drawn in with ropes attached to the prow. They are being unloaded by porters, who wade up to their knees into the sea, and wear shoulder-pads very like those in use in Syrian ports at the present day. Bales of goods, bronze cauldrons, trays perhaps containing ivory, and other objects of value (Pl. XIII f.) are being carried in procession before the king (Pl. XV). All the Phoenicians wear pointed skull-caps, those of the better class having turban-cloths rolled tightly round them. Behind the king (Pl. XV–XVIII) chariots, cavalry, and infantry are advancing from an Assyrian camp.

Lower Register: *The capture of Khazazu.* The city of Khazazu, built upon a *tell* or artificial mound, is shown on Plate XVI. On one side its assault by Assyrian sappers and archers is indicated, while the flames rising from the rest of the town proclaim its fate after capture. The slaughter of the inhabitants is portrayed on Plate XVII f. On Plates XIV–XVI rows of male and female captives are being led before the king. The royal chariot is in attendance, followed by an escort of chariots advancing from an Assyrian camp (Pl. XIII f.).

[1] See above, p. 18. This image was in addition to that which, as the text relates, he sculptured in the Lebanon beside that of Ankhirbe.

PLATES XIX–XXIV.

BAND IV. CAMPAIGN IN NORTHERN SYRIA, 858 B.C.

Texts: The inscription in the field of the upper register (Pl. XIX f.) reads: 'The smiting of Dabigu, the city of Akhuni, the son of Adini.' The lower register has no inscription, but it evidently depicts the sack of a neighbouring town. The capture of Dabigu, one of the tributary cities of Til-Barsip, is recorded in the Monolith-Inscription, Rev., ll. 13–18, as follows: 'In my eponymy, the year of my name, on the 13th of Iyyar I departed from Nineveh. I crossed the Tigris and passed through the lands of Khasamu and Dikhnunu; to Til-Barsip, the stronghold of Akhuni, the son of Adini, I drew nigh. Akhuni, the son of Adini, put his trust in the multitude of his troops and attacked me. I defeated him; I shut him up in [his city]. From Til-Barsip I departed; on rafts of inflated skins I crossed the Euphrates in its time of flood. The cities of [. . . . . a]ga, Tagi[. .], Sûrunu, Paripa, Til-Basherê and Dabigu, six strongholds of Akhuni, the son of Adini, I [stormed], I captured. His numerous fighting-men I slew; their spoil I carried off; two hundred cities, which were round about them, I destroyed, I ravaged, I burned with fire.' In the short summary of the campaign on the Black Obelisk, ll. 32–35, Dabigu is the only city of Akhuni whose capture is recorded,—a testimony to its importance: 'In the second year of my reign I drew nigh to Til-Barsip; the cities of Akhuni, the son of Adini, I captured, and in his city I shut him up. I crossed the Euphrates in its time of flood, and Dabigu, a fortress of the land of Khatti, together with the cities which were round about it, I captured.'

Upper Register: *The storming of the city of Dabigu.* The city of Dabigu, protected by a double line of battlemented walls and flanking towers, is being attacked by sappers, mail-clad archers, and archers mounted in chariots (Pl. XXI–XXIV). Shalmaneser is shown in Plate XX, seated within his pavilion in the Assyrian camp beyond the outer line of investment. Reserve forces of infantry and chariots are depicted on Plate XIX f.

Lower Register: *Shalmaneser watching an assault on a Syrian city.* The king surrounded by his suite is seated on a low hill (Pl. XX), from which he watches the assault on a city (Pl. XX f.), very like to that in the upper register, with the addition of beehive roofs visible above the walls. The attack is being delivered by archers, sappers, and a six-wheeled battering-ram. Within sight of the walls are a number of impaled captives (Pl. XXI), and behind the king are chariots advancing from an Assyrian camp (Pl. XIX f.). On Plates XXII–XXIV rows of male and female prisoners, headed by a saddle-mule and two dromedaries, are being conducted towards another city in Assyrian occupation (Pl. XXIV).

PLATES XXV–XXX.

BAND V. CAMPAIGN IN NORTHERN SYRIA, 858 B.C.

TEXTS. The inscription on the field of the upper register (Pl. XXVIII) reads: 'The tribute of the Un[ḳi]ans.' These people we may probably identify with the inhabitants of Patini, whose submission is recorded on the Monolith, Col. II, ll. 21–4, as follows: 'From Ka[. . . .]shun, of the land of Patini, I received three talents of gold, one hundred talents of silver, three hundred talents of bronze, three hundred talents of iron, one thousand vessels of bronze, one thousand garments of brightly coloured cloth and linen, his daughter [. . . .] with her rich dowry, twenty talents of purple cloth, five hundred oxen and five hundred sheep.' The lower register has no inscription, but, as the scene includes the presentation of a Syrian princess before the king, it may continue the tribute of the King of Unḳi, who gave his daughter to Shalmaneser (*see* above); or it may perhaps portray the tribute of Khaiânu, the son of Gabbari, who dwelt at the foot of Mt. Amanus, and, as we learn from the Monolith, Rev., ll. 24–7, gave his daughter to the King.

UPPER REGISTER: *The tribute of the Unḳians.* From two Syrian cities, standing on the banks of rivers or surrounded by moats (Pl. XXV and XXVII), inhabitants are carrying tribute into the presence of Shalmaneser (Pl. XXVIII); it includes bronze cauldrons, trays possibly of ivory, metal ore or precious stones (represented by 'mountain-lozenges'), sacks of grain, &c. Behind the King chariots and infantry (Pl. XXIX f.) advance from the Assyrian camp on the bank of a river (Pl. XXX). On the farther bank is a fortified city, and a heavy boat with sweeps at either end, like those in use to-day as ferry-boats on the Euphrates, is floating down-stream. Above is a flight of birds, probably duck.

LOWER REGISTER: *Reception by Shalmaneser of a Syrian princess, with her dowry and tribute.* The Syrian princess, the small figure in shoes with points turned up (Pl. XXVIII), is being led by Assyrian officials before Shalmaneser, who stands with his suite before a pavilion in which a feast is prepared (Pl. XXIX). On Plate XXIX f. chariots and infantry advance towards the pavilion from an Assyrian camp. The procession of tribute bearers behind the princess is continued on Plate XXVII, where they are seen to be advancing from their fortified city. The tribute includes horses, bulls, and bronze cauldrons and vessels of different shapes (Pl. XXV–XXVII).

PLATES XXXI–XXXVI.

BAND VI. CAMPAIGN IN NORTHERN SYRIA, 858 B.C.

TEXTS: The inscription in the field of the upper register (Pl. XXXII f.) reads: 'The tribute of Sangara of Carchemish'; and there is no doubt that it is to be taken as covering the scenes in both registers. The Monolith relates how Shalmaneser in the course of his North Syrian campaign ravaged part of Sangar's territory (Rev., ll. 18–20), and later received tribute from him (ll. 27–9). Ll. 18 ff. read: 'From Dabigu I departed and to Sazabê, a stronghold of Sangara of Carchemish, I drew nigh; the city I stormed, I captured; their numerous fighting-men I slew; [. . . . .] as prisoners I carried off. The towns which were round about it I destroyed, I ravaged, I burned with fire.' Ll. 27 ff. read: 'From Sangara of Carchemish I received three talents of gold, seventy talents of silver, thirty talents of bronze, one hundred talents of iron, twenty talents of purple cloth, five hundred weapons, his daughter with (her) dowry, one hundred daughters of his nobles, five hundred oxen and five thousand sheep. One maneh of gold, one talent of silver, two talents of purple cloth, I laid upon him (as tribute), and each year I received them from him.'

UPPER REGISTER: *The tribute of Sangara of Carchemish.* Shalmaneser, followed by military attendants, stands before a royal pavilion, in which wine and food are laid out, and receives an embassy from Sangara of Carchemish (Pl. XXXV). Assyrian officials introduce the two ambassadors followed by bearers of tribute; some carry trays, vessels, and sacks, others bear great tusks of ivory and heavy bronze cauldrons. On Plate XXXII f. the walled city of Carchemish is seen across the Euphrates. On Plate XXXI f. further tribute, including rams and goats, is being brought from another city; this may be intended for a dependent city of Carchemish, or it may possibly be a second representation of Carchemish itself. On Plate XXXV f. Assyrian chariots and infantry advance towards the pavilion and the royal chariot.

LOWER REGISTER: *Reception by Shalmaneser of Sangara's daughter with her dowry and tribute.* Sangara's daughter, followed by servants bearing her dowry, is being led by Assyrian officials before Shalmaneser (Pl. XXXIV). The rest of the scene is very similar to that in the upper register. It may be noted that horses and bulls are here included in the tribute (Pl. XXXIII), and that the scene is closed on the right by an Assyrian fortified camp on the bank of a river (Pl. XXXVI).

PLATES XXXVII–XLII.

BAND VII. CAMPAIGN IN ARMENIA, 857 B.C.

TEXTS: The inscription in the field of the upper register (Pl. XXXVIII–XL) reads: 'The city of Arame, the Urartian, I captured.' That in the field of the lower register (Pl. XL) reads: 'The tribute of the men of Gilzani.' The Gate-Inscription, Col. II, l. 5–Col. III, l. 3, refers to the subjects of this register.[1] Its record may be supplemented from the Monolith-Inscription, Rev., ll. 47–54; this passage gives the following account of the capture of Arṣashku, the city of Arame, which is pictured in the upper register: 'From Daiaene I departed and to Arṣashku, the royal city of Arramu, the Urartian, I drew nigh. Before the splendour of my mighty weapons and my terrible onslaught Arramu, the Urartian, was terrified; he forsook his city and went up into the mountain of Adduri. I went up into the mountain after him and fought a mighty battle in the midst of the mountains. Three thousand, four hundred of his warriors I overthrew with the sword; I rained destruction upon them like the Storm-god. With their blood I dyed the mountain like red wool. I took his camp from him; his chariots, his chargers, his horses, his swift mules, his property, his spoil, and his great possessions I brought back from the midst of the mountains. Arramu, to save his life, climbed a steep mountain. In the strength of my manhood I trampled down his land like a wild bull, his cities I turned into ruins. Arṣashku, together with the cities which were round about it, I destroyed, I ravaged, I burned with fire. I piled up heaps of heads opposite his city-gate. Some I buried alive in the heaps; others I impaled on stakes round about the heaps.' The passage on the Monolith, Rev., ll. 60–2, which records the tribute of Gilzani, depicted on the lower register, reads: '[From the shore of the sea (*i.e.*, Lake Van)] I departed and I drew nigh to the land of Gilzâni. Asâu, King of Gilzâni, with his brethren and his sons, came out to me. Royal [. . . . .], horses broken to the yoke, oxen, sheep, wine, (and) seven two-humped dromedaries, I received from him.' The Black Obelisk, ll. 42–4, gives the following brief summary, in which the subjects of both registers are referred to: 'The lands of Alzi, Sukh[ni], Daiaeni, Nimme, Arṣashkunu, the royal city of Arame, the Urartian, and the lands of Gilzani and Khubushkia (I conquered).' The short account in the Bull-Inscription, ll. 55–9 for the upper register, and ll. 59–60 for the lower register, are very broken, only a few words at the beginnings and ends of lines being preserved.

UPPER REGISTER: *Capture of Arṣashku, the city of Arame, the Urartian.* Assyrian sappers are represented setting fire to the city with brands or torches (Pl. XXXIX), while cavalry and infantry are engaged in the slaughter of Urartians, who advance into battle from the mountains (Pl. XXXVII–XXXIX). Further scenes of slaughter and mutilation

[1] See above, p. 17 f.

are portrayed on Plates XL–XLII, where Shalmaneser is perhaps represented as leading his chariots to the attack. The Urartian warriors may be compared with those on Bands I and II.

Lower Register: *The tribute of the men of Gilzani.* Shalmaneser stands before a royal pavilion which is pitched in the mountains (Pl. XLI), while Assyrian officials present to him men bringing tribute from Gilzani. This includes dromedaries and bulls (Pl. XL), horses (Pl. XXXIX), goats, and sheep (Pl. XXXVII f.). A double-walled city of Gilzani, standing on high ground above a river, shuts in the register on the left (Pl. XXXVII). On the right (Pl. XLI f.), Assyrian infantry and chariots are shown marching over the mountains from camp.

PLATES XLIII–XLVII.

BAND VIII. CAMPAIGN IN NORTH-EAST MESOPOTAMIA, 855 B.C.

Texts: The inscription in the field of the upper register reads: 'Uburi, the city of Ankhiti, the Shubrian, I captured.' The lower register has no inscription, but it is obvious that its scenes refer to the same event. A record of this campaign is given in the following brief summary upon the Black Obelisk, ll. 52–4: 'In the fifth year of my reign I climbed the mountains of Kashiarê; the strongholds I captured; Ankhiti, the Shubrian, I shut up in his city, his rich tribute I received from him.' The account on the Bull-Inscription, ll. 66–7, tallies with that on the Black Obelisk, except that it gives the number of strongholds captured as eleven.

Upper Register: *The capture of Uburi, the city of Ankhiti, the Shubrian.* Shalmaneser, who has descended from his chariot, receives two messengers bringing him news of the assault on Uburi (Pl. XLIII). The city, with its high walls and flanking towers, is built on very undulating ground, and is being attacked by Assyrian archers, who have captured and occupied its outermost fortifications (Pl. XLIV). Archers in chariots attack the city from the other side (Pl. XLV–XLVII).

Lower Register: *The capture of Uburi, continued.* The Assyrian besieging force, part of which operates on higher ground, is continued on Plate XLIII. The apparently deserted city on Plate XLIV, bears a strong resemblance to Uburi in the upper register, with which it may probably be identified. Its capture is indicated by the rows of heads fixed to one of its tall towers. From it male and female prisoners are being led under armed escort to a smaller city in the plain in Assyrian occupation (Pl. XLV–XLVII). It should be noted that one section is wanting from the left end of the band, which may be partly restored, in the lower register, from two fragments not in the British Museum (cf. Unger, *Zum Bronzetor von Balawat*, Tafel I). This shows Shalmaneser meeting Assyrian officers who have brought him news of the city's capture; a mounted messenger, on his way to head-quarters, is seen crossing the hills on Pl. XLIII.

PLATES XLVIII–LIII.

BAND IX. CAMPAIGN IN SYRIA (HAMATH), 854 B.C.

TEXTS: There are two inscriptions in the field of the upper register. The one, on Plate XLIX f., reads: 'The city of Pargâ I captured'; the other, on Plate LII f., reads: 'Adâ, a city of Urkhileni[1] of the land of Hamath, I captured.' The inscription in the field of the lower register (Pl. L) reads: 'Ḳarḳara, the city of Urkhilêni of the land of Hamath, I captured.' The Monolith, Rev., ll. 87–101, gives the following account of the campaign in Hamath and the famous battle of Ḳarḳar: 'From Aleppo I departed and I drew nigh to the cities of Irkhuleni of Hamath. Ardennu, Pargâ, and Arganâ, his royal city, I captured. His spoil, his property, the possessions of his palaces I brought forth, and to his palaces I set fire. From Arganâ I departed and I drew nigh to Ḳarḳara. Ḳarḳara, his royal city, I destroyed, I ravaged, I burned with fire.' After enumerating the names of Irkhuleni's allies, headed by Adad-'idri of Damascus, and the forces they brought with them, the text proceeds: 'These twelve kings came to his aid, to wage war and battle they advanced against me. With the exalted forces, which the lord Ashur had bestowed, with the mighty weapons which Nergal had presented, I fought with them and from Ḳarḳara up to Gilzau I defeated them. Fourteen thousand of their warriors I overthrew with the sword, and like the Storm-god I rained destruction upon them. I scattered their corpses; with their numerous troops I filled the ruins, and with the sword I caused their blood to flow down the ravines of the district. There was little space for completing their destruction; the broad plain was used up for their burial. With their bodies I dammed the Orontes like a . . . . . In that battle I took from them their chariots, their chargers, and their horses trained to the yoke.' In the brief summary of the battle given by the Black Obelisk, ll. 57–66, the number of the slain is put at 20,500. The Bull-Inscription, ll. 71–4, contains a similarly short account, in which the enemy's loss is put at 25,000 men. The pursuit is also stated to have been continued on the sea, the passage concluding: 'To save their lives they fled; I embarked in ships, I journeyed into the midst of the sea.'

UPPER REGISTER: *The capture of the cities of Pargâ and Adâ in Hamath.* The two scenes in the register are divided from each other by the Assyrian camp on Plate LI. To the left the city of Pargâ is being fiercely attacked by archers, while a huge battering-ram makes a breach in the wall (Pl. L). On Plate XLVIII f. Assyrian archers, mounted on horses and in chariots, are shooting down the warriors of Hamath at the gallop. On

[1] The name of this King of Hamath is written in several ways: on this band as Urkhileni and Urkhilêni, on the Monolith-Inscription as Irkhuleni, and on Band XIII (see below, p. 34) as Irkhulêni.

Plate LII f. similar scenes are portrayed at the assault upon Adâ, another city of Irkhuleni, and Shalmaneser is shown in his chariot leading the attack. Here the storming-parties are gaining access to the city by means of ladders planted against the walls.

Lower Register: *The capture of the city of Ḳarḳara.* On Plate XLVIII f. the city of Ḳarḳara is seen in flames, while Assyrian officers watch the conflagration from a neighbouring plantation of fruit-trees, through which runs an irrigation-stream. On Plate L f. captives and spoil from Ḳarḳara are being led before Shalmaneser, who is seated in a pavilion (Pl. LII). Behind the pavilion the royal chariot and escort are drawn up, and the register is closed by the Assyrian camp on the bank of a stream (Pl. LIII).

PLATES LIV–LIX.

BAND X. EXPEDITION TO THE SOURCE OF THE TIGRIS, 853 B.C.

Texts: Though there is no inscription in the field of the upper register, it is clear that both registers relate to the same expedition. The inscription in the field of the curved portion of the lower register (Pl. LV f.) reads: 'Kulisi, the royal city of Mutzuata, I captured, I burned with fire.' That in the field of the flat portion of the same register (Pl. LVIII f.) reads: 'I entered the sources of the river; I offered sacrifices to the gods; my royal image I set up.' The Black Obelisk, ll. 67–72, gives the following account of this expedition: 'In the seventh year of my reign I marched against the cities of Khabini of Til-abni. Til-abni, his stronghold, together with the cities which were round about it, I captured. I marched to the source of the Tigris, the place where the water comes forth. I cleansed the weapon of Ashur therein; I took victims for my gods; I held a joyful feast. A mighty image of my majesty I fashioned; the glory of Ashur, my lord, my deeds of valour, all I had accomplished in the lands, I inscribed thereon and I set it up there.' The Bull-Inscription, ll. 75–7, gives a very similar account of the expedition. It supplies the additional detail that Shalmaneser not only captured the cities round Til-abni, but destroyed them with fire; and, after the record of the sacrifices at the head of the Tigris, it adds (l. 77): 'The cities which had not submitted to Ashur I overthrew with the sword; the tribute of the land of Nairi I received.'

Upper Register: *Submission of a local chief to Shalmaneser; and sacrificial scene.* The greater part of the register is taken up with the submission of the local chief. An Assyrian force of infantry, cavalry, and chariots (Pl. LIV–LVI) forms an escort to a body of officials who present the deputation to the king (Pl. LVII), before whom its members kneel and kiss the ground. Behind the king's body-guard is the royal chariot, followed by an escort of chariots and infantry (Pl. LVIII f.). The closing section of the register (Pl. LIX), in which the figures face the other way, is occupied with a sacrificial scene, which is to be taken as forming part of the ceremonial at the source of the Tigris, the principal incidents of which are portrayed in the flat portion of the lower register (see below).

LOWER REGISTER: *The capture of Kulisi; and scenes at the source of the Tigris.* Shalmaneser, accompanied by an infantry escort, advances in his chariot from the Assyrian camp (Pl. LIV f.) and is met by a messenger who brings tidings of the fall of Kulisi. On Plate LVI the city is seen in flames, and its inhabitants after mutilation are being beheaded or impaled. The flat portion of the register (Pl. LVII–LIX) represents the arrival of Shalmaneser at the natural tunnel in the limestone hills through which the Bylkalein-Su, one of the head-streams of the Tigris, flows in its upper course. An Assyrian force of infantry, cavalry, and chariots advances up the left bank of the shallow stream (Pl. LVII f.). The king, having left his chariot, has mounted a horse and, followed by his body-guard on foot, has just crossed the stream at the mouth of the gorge through which it emerges into the plain (Pl. LVIII). A bull and a ram are being led forward for sacrifice before the image of Shalmaneser, which is being carved on the rock-face of the grotto, in front of the tunnel's mouth, by a sculptor standing on a block in the stream (Pl. LIX). The subterranean course of the river is conventionally shown by means of rectangular openings, through which men are seen wading waist-deep and carrying plants or torches. The trees, which appear to be growing in the stream and protruding from the openings, explain the convention: at a point near its mouth the roof of the tunnel has fallen in, and one can still look down on to the stream from above through a wide opening, on the steep sides of which brushwood and small trees have found a footing. A sentry on the hill above the natural tunnel closes the register. The sacrificial scene in the Upper Register (Pl. LIX) is taking place at the head of a neighbouring valley. The objects which are usually explained as four rows of posts across the valley, may perhaps be altars of incense, the rising smoke from which is represented conventionally by disks.

PLATES LX–LXV.

BAND XI. CAMPAIGN IN SOUTHERN BABYLONIA, 851 B.C.

TEXTS: The inscription in the field of the upper register (Pl. LXI f.), which is to be taken as giving the subject of the whole band, reads: 'The tribute of Adini, son of Dakuri,[1] the Chaldean.' The Gate-Inscription, Col. IV, l. 1–Col. VI, l. 8, refers to this campaign and describes in some detail how Shalmaneser, after quelling Marduk-bêl-usâte's revolt in Babylonia, offered sacrifices in Babylon and Borsippa, and then marched southwards and received the tribute of the Chaldeans.[2] The Black Obelisk, ll. 73–84, gives the following

[1] *I. e.*, of Bît-Dakuri, a 'Dakurian'.

[2] See above, pp. 18 ff.

account of the march into Chaldea and the events which preceded it: 'In the eighth year of my reign against Marduk-shum-iddina, King of Karduniash, his younger brother, Marduk-bêl-usâte, revolted; they divided (the land) into two camps. To avenge (*i. e.*, assist) Marduk-shum-iddina I marched; I captured the city of Mê-turnat. In the ninth year of my reign I marched to Akkad a second time; I besieged Gananate. As for Marduk-bêl-usâte, with the fear of Ashur's splendour did Marduk overwhelm him, and to save his life he went up into the mountains. I pursued him, and Marduk-bêl-usâte, together with the rebels who were with him, I overthrew with the sword. I marched to the great cities; I made sacrifices in Babylon, Borsippa, and Cuthah; I offered offerings to the great gods. I went down to the land of Chaldea; I captured their cities. The tribute of the kings of Chaldea I received. Terror of my arms overwhelmed (the country) to the Persian Gulf.' The Bull-Inscription, ll. 78–84, gives a very similar account, mentioning the city of Lakhiru as captured along with Mê-turnat. The portion of the text (ll. 82–4), which relates to the march into Chaldea, reads: 'I went down to Chaldea, I conquered their cities. To the sea, which they call Marratu,[1] I marched. The tribute of Adini, son of Dakuri, (and) of Mushallim-Marduk, son of Ukani, silver, gold, ushû-wood and ivory, I received in Babylon.'

Upper Register: *The tribute of Adini, the Chaldean.* Shalmaneser, having descended from his chariot, receives on foot the tribute of Adini, which he has sent in the charge of two ambassadors, who raise their hands in token of submission (Pl. LXII). As on other bands, the deputation is introduced into the King's presence by a group of Assyrian officials. Behind the King's chariot and body-guard, the royal escort of chariots, infantry, and cavalry crosses a stream by a bridge of boats and advances through date-plantations (Pl. LX f.). In the curved part of the band Dakurians are seen bearing tribute from their city and ferrying it in boats across a river (Pl. LXIII–LXV). The tribute includes small vessels, possibly ivory borne on a tray, bronze cauldrons, bales of goods, and a heavy object carried on the shoulders of two porters, perhaps a trunk of ushû-wood.

Lower Register: *The tribute of the Chaldeans.* Shalmaneser, who has left camp with a force of chariots, cavalry, and infantry, approaches a bridge of boats over a stream (Pl. LX f.); the head of the column, which has already crossed, meets some Chaldeans (Pl. LXII). The latter are bringing tribute, including two oxen, from their city, while women watch their departure from the walls (Pl. LXIII). Beyond the city a high Assyrian official, seated on a carved stool, watches the collection of bronze vessels and other tribute at a bridge over a stream (Pl. LXIV). The register is closed by a group of three Chaldeans shooting birds in a date-plantation (Pl. LXV).

[1] 'The Bitter Water,' *i. e.*, the Persian Gulf, so called from its salt water.

PLATES LXVI–LXXI.

BAND XII. CAMPAIGN IN NORTHERN SYRIA, 850 B.C.

TEXTS: The inscription in the field of the upper register (Pl. LXIX) reads: 'Arnê, the city of Arame, I captured.' That in the field of the lower register (Pl. LXX) reads: '[. . . . .]agdâ, the city of Arame, son of Gusi, I captured.' The Black Obelisk, l. 85 f., gives the following brief account of the campaign in which Arnê was captured: 'In the tenth year of my reign I crossed the Euphrates for the eighth time. The cities of Sangara of Carchemish I conquered. To the cities of Arame I drew nigh; Arnê, his royal city, together with a hundred of its cities, I captured.' The Bull-Inscription, ll. 84–7, gives a parallel account, with a few variants in the conventional phraseology. It is probable that the lower register refers to events of this campaign (see below); but it may possibly depict episodes in the Syrian campaign of the following year, 849 B.C., in the course of which cities of Arame were captured. The Bull-Inscription, l. 90 f., reads: 'In the eleventh year of my reign I departed from Nineveh. For the ninth time I crossed the Euphrates in its time of flood; ninety-seven cities of Sangar I captured; one hundred cities of Arame I captured, I destroyed, I devasted, I burned with fire.' After describing how he invaded Hamath (cf. Band XIII) and defeated Adad-'idri of Damascus and his allies, the Bull-Inscription, l. 94 f., continues: 'On my return I captured Apparazu, the stronghold of Arame.'

UPPER REGISTER: *The capture of Arnê, the royal city of Arame.* The city, the walls of which are defended by bowmen, is shown on Pl. LXIX; it is being attacked on both sides by Assyrian archers, some of whom are in chariots (Pl. LXVI–LXVIII, and LXIX–LXXI), under Shalmaneser's leadership (Pl. LXX). In the right-hand section of the attack slain archers from the city lie prone beneath the horses (Pl. LXIX–LXXI). The register is closed on the right by the Assyrian camp (LXXI).

LOWER REGISTER: *The conquest of other cities of Arame.* The register is divided into two scenes by the Assyrian camp on Pl. LXIX. In the left-hand scene (Pl. LXVI–LXVIII) an armed Assyrian escort is conducting a column of male and female captives, with spoil of herds and flocks, from their city to the Assyrian camp. In the right-hand scene a fortified city, the name of which is broken (see above), is being attacked by archers, some of whom shoot from chariots under Shalmaneser's leadership (LXIX). Wounded warriors from the city lie in various attitudes beneath the horses (Pl. LXIX–LXXI). To judge by analogy from other Bands we may probably connect this register directly with the upper one, and regard the cities represented as two of the hundred cities of Arame, captured at the same time as Arnê, in 850 B.C. (see above).

PLATES LXXII–LXXVII.

BAND XIII. CAMPAIGN IN SYRIA (HAMATH), 849 B. C.

TEXTS: The inscription in the field of the upper register (Pl. LXXII–LXXIV), which gives the subject of the whole Band, reads 'Ashtamaku, the royal city of Irkhulêni of [Ha]math, together with eighty-six cities, I captured'. The Black Obelisk, ll. 87–88, includes the following short summary of this portion of the campaign of 849 B. C.: 'In the eleventh year of my reign I crossed the Euphrates for the ninth time and captured cities without number. To the cities of Khatti, of Hamath, I went down, and eighty-nine cities I captured.' The text then goes on to record the defeat of Adad-idri and his allies. The Bull-Inscription, after describing the conquest of Arame's hundred cities (see above, Band XII), continues in l. 91 f.: 'The flank of Mt. Amanus I held; I crossed over Mt. Iaraḳu; to the cities of Hamath I went down. Ashtamaku, together with ninety-nine cities, I captured; I slew their people, I carried off their spoil.'

UPPER REGISTER: *The capture of Ashtamaku and two other cities of Hamath.* The register contains three scenes; the first two are separated from each other by the Assyrian camp on Plate LXXIII, the third beginning with the chariots on Plate LXXV. Each scene represents an attack on a separate city, that on Plate LXXII f. being Ashtamaku, the royal city of Irkhulêni. Two of Irkhulêni's three-horse chariots, which have fled from the battle outside the walls, have just reached the city, in spite of spent horses and damaged wheels. They are pursued by Assyrian chariots and cavalry, who shoot as they gallop across the plain strewn with the dead. Ashtamaku is still being assaulted by archers, but is on the point of surrendering. The city in the second scene (Pl. LXXV), which is surrounded by trees on the bank of a stream, is being assaulted by sappers with scaling-ladders, while Assyrian archers continue to shoot from a distance; they are supported by chariots (Pl. LXXIV), in the first of which is the King. The city in the third scene is smaller and is surrounded by a single wall (Pl. LXXVII). A figure raises a hand in token of surrender, while he points to the aged ruler of the city, who reclines on a couch in the presence of his women; by a legitimate convention the engraver has represented the whole of this episode as taking place upon the wall.

LOWER REGISTER: *Shalmaneser's reception of prisoners from a captured city of Hamath.* The King (Pl. LXXIII), who has left his royal pavilion and the Assyrian camp (Pl. LXXII), has descended from his chariot and stands surrounded by his personal attendants and body-guard, while the ruler of the city does obeisance at his feet. The rest of the scene (Pl. LXXIV–LXXVII), is taken up with files of male and female captives, who are being escorted from their city by Assyrian infantry, cavalry, and chariots. The city is unlike the other cities of Hamath, since its walls are without battlements, and peaked roofs protect its gates and their flanking towers from the weather.

APPENDIX

THE GATES OF ASHUR-NAṢIR-PAL (PLATES LXXVIII–LXXX).

PLATE LXXVIII.

BAND I. ASHUR-NAṢIR-PAL RECEIVING CAPTIVES FROM THE CITY OF ELIPI.

TEXTS: The text which is engraved in the upper field of the register, behind the king and above his chariot and body-guard, reads: [cuneiform], 'Palace of Ashur-naṣir-pal, King of the world, King of Assyria, the son of Tukulti-Ninib, King of Assyria, the son of Adad-nirari, King of Assyria.' That which is engraved above the Assyrian officials, who are introducing captives into the King's presence, reads: [cuneiform] [. . . . .], 'Captives from Elipi, the city of [. . . . .].' It should be noted that the portion of the band, which is preserved, ends with the Assyrian official who raises his hand, pointing to the captives behind him. The portion of the band on which the captives were engraved, and on which the text was continued, is wanting; the three joined fragments above, engraved with a raised hand, and the heads of two horses, as well as the detached piece of border below, were incorrectly affixed by the original restorer of the bronze and do not actually form parts of the band.

REGISTER: Ashur-naṣir-pal, accompanied by the royal chariot and body-guard, stands under a light canopy and receives a deputation of Assyrian officials, who are introducing into his presence captives from the conquered city of Elipi. The line of captives was engraved on the curved portion of the band, which encircled the cylindrical shaft of the door, but is now entirely wanting.

PLATES LXXIX, LXXX.

BAND II. ASHUR-NAṢIR-PAL AT THE CONQUEST OF A CITY OF BÎT-IAKHIRI.

Text: The text, which is engraved in the upper field of the register reads: [cuneiform] [..........] [cuneiform][1] [cuneiform], '[..........]su a city of Bît-Iakhiri, I captured.'

Register: Ashur-naṣir-pal, shooting from his chariot, is leading an attack upon the city, from each side of which a sortie has been made by the garrison. The defenders, standing below the wall of their city, shoot on the Assyrians as they approach, while women watch the battle from the walls. Other defenders fall in their flight before the chariots. The scene is closed on the right by a third Assyrian chariot advancing to the attack. This band, though broken in places, enables us to ascertain the breadth of Ashir-naṣir-pal's doors, since no part is missing from either end of it. It will be noticed that in both bands the figures are isolated, and little skill is shown in composition and grouping. In this respect they present an interesting contrast to the best work of Shalmaneser's reign, in which considerable ingenuity is often shown in producing a rich effect by the massing of figures and the variety of their design.

[1] This character is not completely preserved.

NOTE ON THE SCALE OF REPRODUCTION EMPLOYED IN THE PLATES

In order to avoid rendering the volume unwieldy, it has been necessary in the Collotype Plates to reproduce the bands on a scale less than the full size of the originals. For the Gates of Shalmaneser, on Plates I–LXXVII, that adopted is slightly over half-scale; the ratio is approximately 1 : 0·54. The two bands from the Gates of Ashur-naṣir-pal, published in the Appendix, are reproduced half-scale.

PLATE II

VICTIMS FOR SACRIFICE; AND ASSYRIAN CHARIOTS AND ARCHERS

BAND I. 2. CAMPAIGN IN ARMENIA, 860 B.C. (*continued*).

Upper Register: Victims for sacrifice before Shalmaneser's image; the royal chariot and bodyguard.
Lower Register: Chariots in reserve and archers at the storming of Sugunia.

British Museum.—Photo. Oxford University Press.

PLATE III

ASSYRIAN CHARIOTS CROSSING THE ARMENIAN MOUNTAINS; AND THE CAPTURE OF SUGUNIA

PLATE III

BAND I. 3. CAMPAIGN IN ARMENIA, 860 B.C. (*continued*).

Upper Register : Chariots of the royal escort crossing the mountains.
Lower Register : The storming and capture of the city of Sugunia.

British Museum.—Photo. Oxford University Press.

PLATE IV

ASSYRIAN CHARIOTS AND CAVALRY; AND CAPTIVES FROM SUGUNIA

BAND I. 4. CAMPAIGN IN ARMENIA, 860 B.C. (*continued*).

Upper Register : Chariots and cavalry, forming part of the royal escort.
Lower Register : Yoked captives from Sugunia.

British Museum.—Photo. Oxford University Press.

PLATE V

ASSYRIAN CAVALRY AND INFANTRY; AND CAPTIVES FROM SUGUNIA

BAND I. 5. CAMPAIGN IN ARMENIA, 860 B.C. (*continued*).

Upper Register : Cavalry and infantry, forming part of the royal escort.
Lower Register : Captives from Sugunia led before a high Assyrian officer.

British Museum.—Photo. Oxford University Press.

PLATE VI

ASSYRIAN FORTIFIED CAMP AND CHARIOTS

BAND I. 6. CAMPAIGN IN ARMENIA, 860 B.C. (*continued*).

Upper Register: Assyrian fortified camp, showing royal pavilion and the baking of bread.
Lower Register: Assyrian chariots and officer.

PLATE VII

CAPTURED CITY OF URARTU WITH IMPALED INHABITANTS

BAND II. 1. CAMPAIGN IN ARMENIA, 860 B.C. (*continued*).

Upper Register: Booty from a captured city of Urartu; impaled inhabitants.
Lower Register: Assyrian chariots and cavalry at the storming of a city of Urartu.

British Museum.—Photo. Oxford University Press.

PLATE VIII

BURNING OF A CITY OF URARTU AND DESTRUCTION OF ITS DATE-PLANTATIONS

BAND II. 2. CAMPAIGN IN ARMENIA, 860 B.C. (*continued*).

Upper Register: Burning of a city of Urartu, and cutting down of its date-plantations.
Lower Register: Assyrian chariots and archers at the storming of a city of Urartu.

Gates of Shalmaneser.

British Museum.—Photo. Oxford University Press.

PLATE IX

SLAUGHTER OF URARTIANS; AND CAPTURE OF ONE OF THEIR CITIES

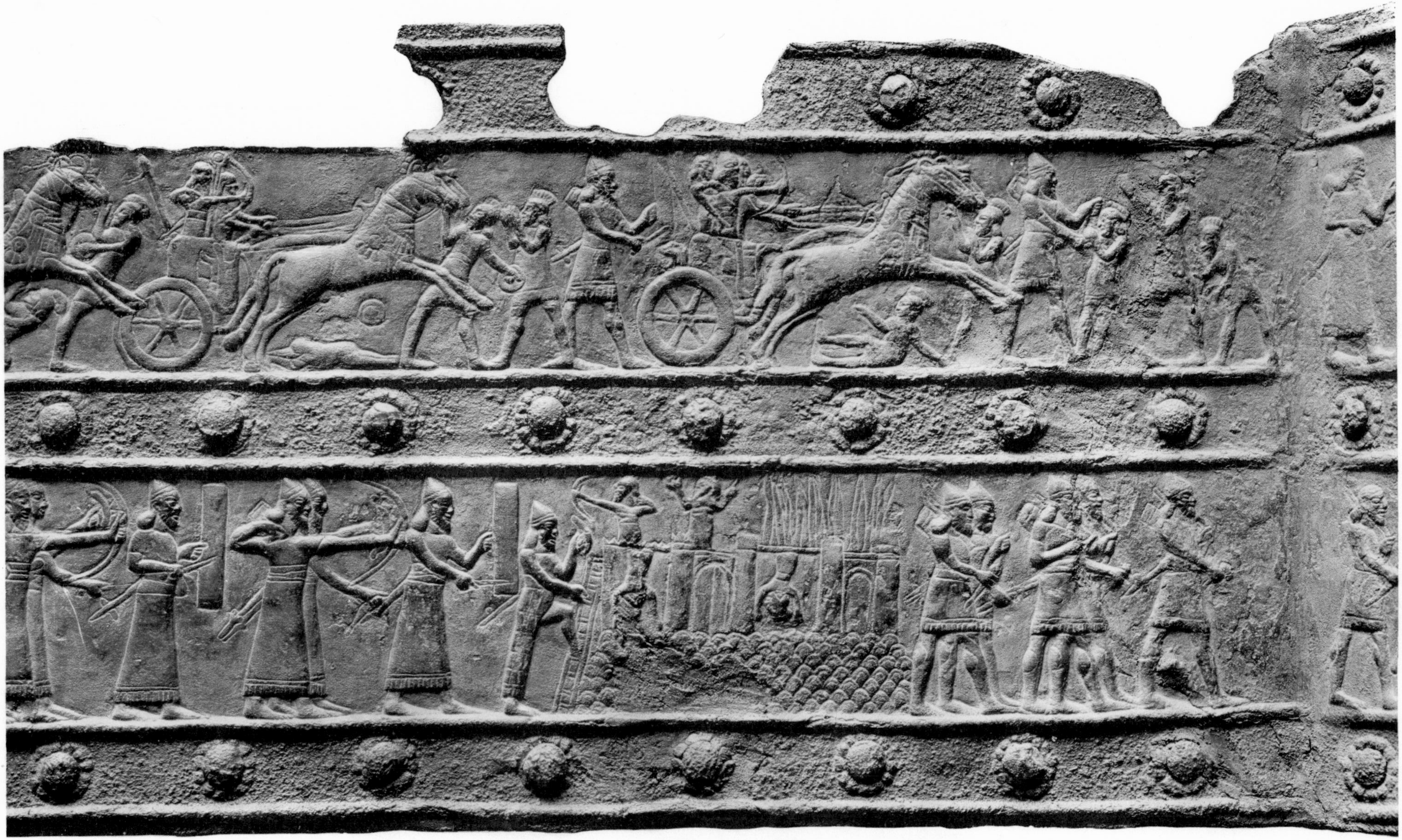

BAND II. 3. CAMPAIGN IN ARMENIA, 860 B.C. (*continued*).

Upper Register : Slaughter of Urartians by Assyrian chariots under Shalmaneser's leadership.
Lower Register : Storming and capture of a city of Urartu.

British Museum.—Photo. Oxford University Press.

PLATE X

SLAUGHTER OF URARTIANS; CAPTURED HORSES AND YOKED PRISONERS

BAND II. 4. CAMPAIGN IN ARMENIA, 860 B.C. (*continued*).

Upper Register : Slaughter of Urartians by Assyrian infantry with bow and sword.
Lower Register : Horses and yoked prisoners from a captured city of Urartu.

British Museum.—Photo. Oxford, University Press.

PLATE XI

URARTIANS ADVANCING INTO BATTLE; AND DISPOSAL OF CAPTIVES

BAND II. 5. CAMPAIGN IN ARMENIA, 860 B.C. (*continued*).

Upper Register : Urartians advancing into battle from the mountains.
Lower Register : Handing over of prisoners to an Assyrian officer from the camp.

British Museum.—Photo. Oxford University Press.

PLATE XII

URARTIANS ADVANCING INTO BATTLE; ASSYRIAN OFFICER AND FORTIFIED CAMP

Band II. 6. Campaign in Armenia, 860 b.c. (*continued*).

Upper Register : Urartians advancing into battle from the mountains.
Lower Register : Assyrian officer and his chariot ; fortified camp.

PLATE XIII

BOATS WITH TRIBUTE FROM TYRE; ASSYRIAN CAMP AND CHARIOTS

BAND III. 1. CAMPAIGN IN PHOENICIA, 859 B. C.

Upper Register : Transport of tribute in boats from Tyre to the mainland.
Lower Register : Assyrian camp and chariots on the expedition against Khazazu.

PLATE XIV

TRIBUTE FROM TYRE AND SIDON; AND CAPTIVES FROM KHAZAZU

BAND III. 2. CAMPAIGN IN PHOENICIA, 859 B.C. (*continued*).

Upper Register: Tribute from Tyre and Sidon, including bales of goods, bronze cauldrons, &c.
Lower Register: Assyrian officials leading captives from Khazazu into the presence of Shalmaneser.

British Museum.—Photo. Oxford University Press.

PLATE XV

SHALMANESER RECEIVING TRIBUTE; AND CAPTIVES FROM KHAZAZU

BAND III. 3. CAMPAIGN IN PHOENICIA, 859 B. C. (*continued*).

Upper Register : Shalmaneser, followed by his bodyguard and chariot, receiving the tribute of Tyre and Sidon.
Lower Register : Captives from Khazazu being led into the king's presence.

British Museum.—Photo. Oxford University Press.

PLATE XVI

ASSYRIAN CHARIOTS IN PHOENICIA; AND THE STORMING OF KHAZAZU

BAND III. 4. CAMPAIGN IN PHOENICIA, 858 B.C. (*continued*).

Upper Register: Assyrian chariots in Phoenicia.
Lower Register: The storming of the city of Khazazu.

British Museum.—Photo. Oxford University Press

PLATE XVII

ASSYRIAN CHARIOTS AND CAVALRY; AND SLAUGHTER OF MEN FROM KHAZAZU

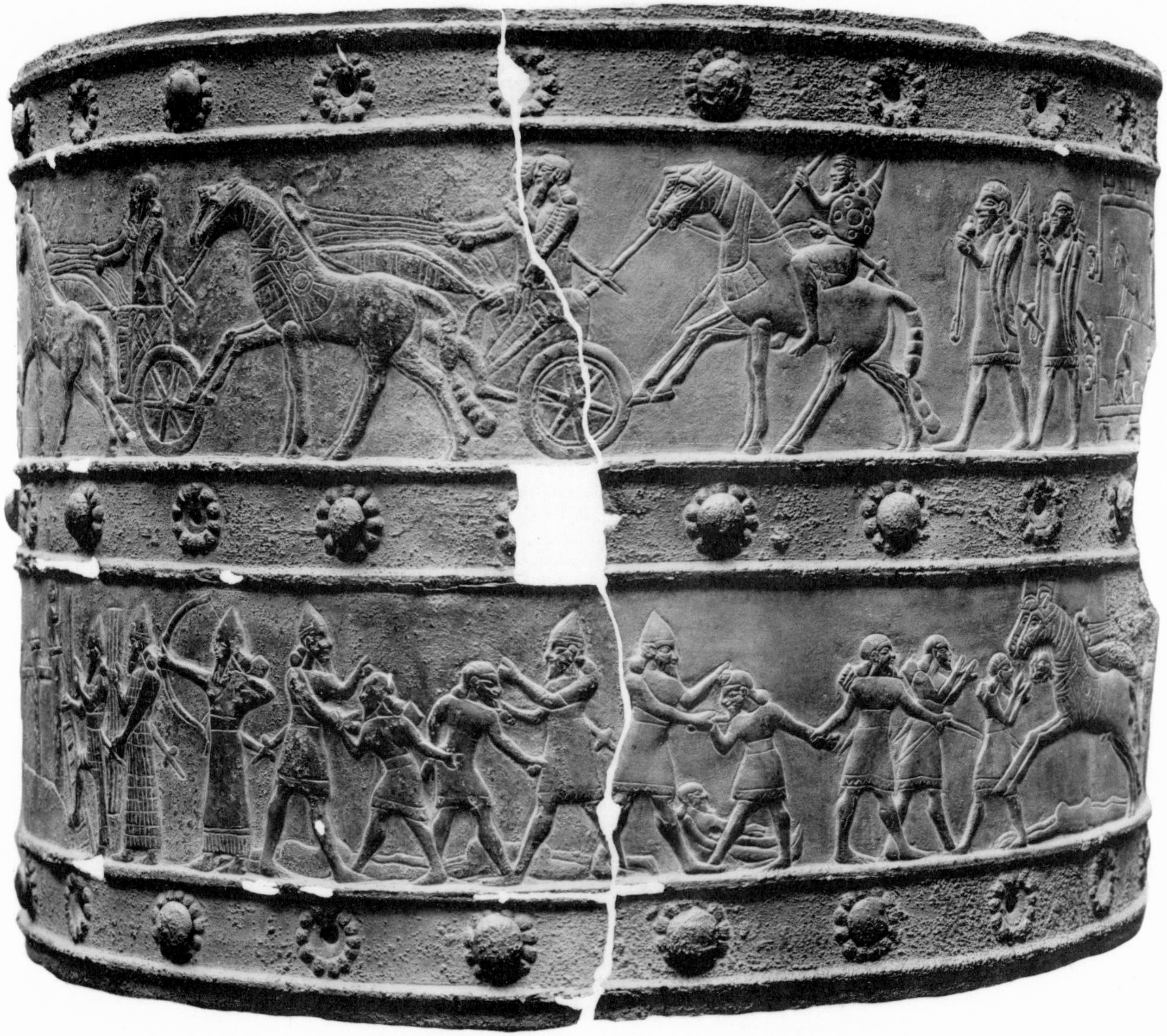

BAND III. 5. CAMPAIGN IN PHOENICIA, 859 B. C. (*continued*).

Upper Register: Assyrian chariots and cavalry; two military officers.
Lower Register: Slaughter of men from Khazazu.

British Museum.—Photo. Oxford University Press.

PLATE XVIII

ASSYRIAN CAVALRY AND CAMP; SLAUGHTER OF MEN FROM KHAZAZU

Band III. 6. Campaign in Phoenicia, 859 B.C. (*continued*).

Upper Register: Assyrian cavalry and two military officers; fortified camp.
Lower Register: Slaughter of men from Khazazu.

British Museum.—Photo. Oxford University Press.

PLATE XIX

ASSYRIAN INFANTRY, CHARIOTS, AND FORTIFIED CAMP

BAND IV. 1. CAMPAIGN IN NORTHERN SYRIA, 858 B.C.

Upper Register : Assyrian infantry and chariots at the storming of Dabigu.
Lower Register : Chariots advancing from an Assyrian camp.

British Museum.—Photo. Oxford University Press.

PLATE XX

SHALMANESER IN CAMP, AND WATCHING AN ASSAULT UPON A CITY

BAND IV. 2. CAMPAIGN IN NORTHERN SYRIA, 858 B.C. (*continued*).

Upper Register: Shalmaneser encamped before the city of Dabigu.
Lower Register: Shalmaneser watching an assault on a city from a neighbouring hill.

British Museum.—Photo. Oxford University Press.

PLATE XXI

THE STORMING OF DABIGU; AND IMPALED SYRIANS OUTSIDE THEIR CITY-WALL

BAND IV. 3. CAMPAIGN IN NORTHERN SYRIA, 858 B.C. (*continued*).

Upper Register: The storming of the city of Dabigu.
Lower Register: Impaled inhabitants outside a city; Assyrian infantry and horses.

British Museum.—Photo. Oxford University Press.

PLATE XXII

ASSYRIAN ARCHERS AND CHARIOTS; AND YOKED CAPTIVES UNDER ESCORT

BAND IV. 4. CAMPAIGN IN NORTHERN SYRIA, 858 B.C. (*continued*).

Upper Register: Assyrian archers and chariots at the storming of Dabigu.
Lower Register: Yoked captives and their Assyrian escort.

British Museum.—Photo. Oxford University Press.

PLATE XXIII

ASSYRIAN ARCHERS AND CHARIOTS; FEMALE CAPTIVES, MULE, AND DROMEDARIES ON THE MARCH

BAND IV. 5. CAMPAIGN IN NORTHERN SYRIA, 858 B. C. (*continued*).

Upper Register : Assyrian archers and chariots at the storming of Dabigu.
Lower Register : Female captives, mule, and dromedaries on the march.

British Museum.—Photo. Oxford University Press.

PLATE XXIV

ASSYRIAN CHARIOTS AND ARCHERS; TRAIN OF CAPTIVES AND SPOIL APPROACHING A CITY IN SYRIA

BAND IV. 6. CAMPAIGN IN NORTHERN SYRIA, 858 B.C. (*continued*).

Upper Register: Assyrian chariots and archers at the storming of Dabigu.
Lower Register: Captives, mule, and dromedaries approaching a Syrian city.

British Museum.—Photo. Oxford University Press.

PLATE XXV

TRIBUTE OF THE UNKIANS AND OF A PRINCE OF SYRIA

Band V. 1. Campaign in Northern Syria, 858 B.C. (*continued*).

Upper Register: Unkians bearing tribute from one of their cities.
Lower Register: Tribute of a Syrian prince and his city.

British Museum.—Photo. Oxford University Press.

PLATE XXVI

TRIBUTE OF THE UNKIANS AND OF A PRINCE OF SYRIA